THE DIRECTORY OF
SIGNS & SIGNALS

THE DIRECTORY OF
SIGNS &
SIGNALS

A Guide to Signs, Codes, and Signals From Across the World

First published in 2004 by
Chartwell Books Inc.
A Division of Book Sales Inc.
114 Northfield Avenue
Edison, New Jersey 08837

ISBN: 0-7858-1902-9

Note from the publisher
This book should be considered as a reference source only and is not
intended to replace instruction or advice from a qualified pracititioner or
other professional. The author and publisher disclaim any liability, loss,
injury, or damage incurred as a consequence, directly or indirectly, of the
use and application of the contents.

This book was conceived, designed, and produced by
THE IVY PRESS LIMITED
The Old Candlemakers
Lewes, East Sussex BN7 2NZ

Creative Director: Peter Bridgewater
Publisher: Sophie Collins
Editorial Director: Jason Hook
Project Editor: Mandy Greenfield
Designer: Richard Constable
Illustrators: Peters & Zabransky Ltd
Picture Research: Vanessa Fletcher

Printed and bound in China

C O N T E N T S

INTRODUCTION
A   WORLD   OF   SIGNS

The world is full of signs: traffic lights, company logos, the letters of the alphabet. All of these signs are abstract—there is no reason why blue should not mean "stop," and there is nothing actually doggish about the word "dog" or the letters D-O-G—but we understand them instantly and instinctively.

There are other sign systems with meanings that are not immediately obvious, or which are known only to specialists. To most people, these signs are like foreign languages or secret codes: you know something is being said, but you don't know what. This book is an introduction to some of the systems of signs and signals that are widely used or that have had an impact on our civilization. Morse code, for example, transformed communications in the 19th century by making it possible to communicate instantly across borders and continents. The effects were at least as profound as the influence of the Internet has been in recent years.

Consider what Morse code is: a means of describing the letters of the alphabet, which are themselves an abstract sign system for describing the sounds of speech, which is in turn a complex system of abstract vocal signs. So every tap of the telegraph key is a sign for a sign for a sign. And Morse is not so much a code as a highly specialized, long-distance way of signing English. Anything that can be written in English can be expressed in Morse code. The same is true of semaphore, and of Braille.

Because most of these signaling systems convey basic information, they are relatively easy to learn and use. *The Directory of Signs & Signals* shows you how. It is organized into five sections, each covering a group of communication systems. "Distance communication" covers sempahore, Morse code, and international maritime signal flags. "Personal communication" includes Braille, sign language, and some of the emoticons now sent by e-mail every day.

"Survival" provides all the essential ground-to-air signals, body signals, and trail signs to use, should you ever need rescuing, while "Sports" covers the hand signals used in American football and soccer, as well as the meanings of the brightly colored flags waved in motor racing. The book ends with a "Miscellaneous" section, which includes the swift gestures used on a busy trading floor and the universally adopted meteorological symbols, which are interpreted for us each day by weather forecasters.

All the sign systems in this book are a testament to human ingenuity, to the irrepressible urge to communicate—no matter how far the distance, no matter what the obstacles, no matter how bald the words. We all want to communicate with one another, and that is why we love to invent signs and signals.

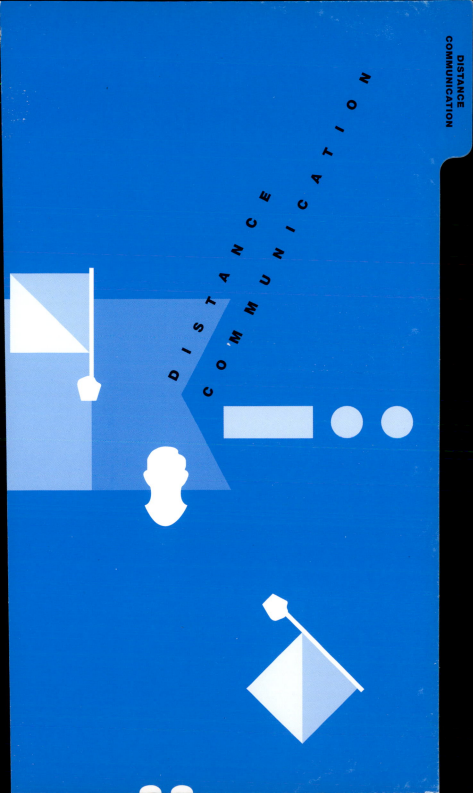

DISTANCE COMMUNICATION

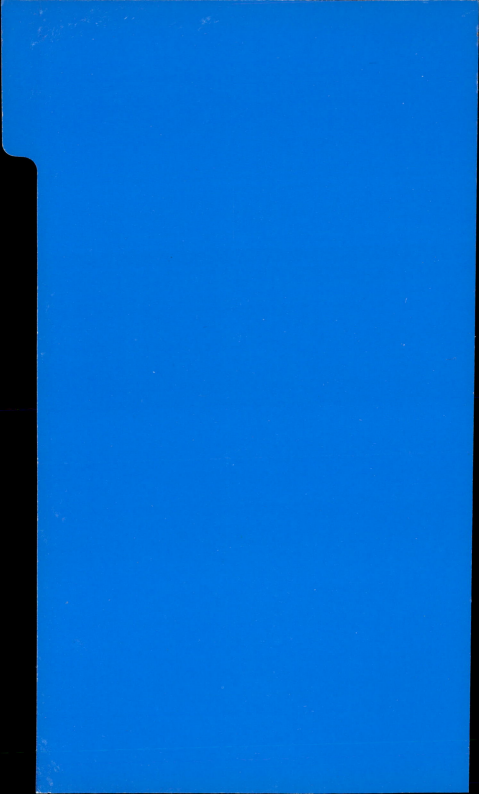

SEMAPHORE

MORSE CODE

**MARITIME
SIGNAL FLAGS**

S E M A P H O R E

Semaphore is a system of long-distance communication that uses two flags to send simple, short-range messages. In semaphore, the user holds a flag in each hand to make his or her movements easily visible to the distant observer. Each flag can be held at arm's length in any one of eight positions: straight up and down, horizontally left and right, diagonally up to the left and right, or diagonally down to the left and right. One can visualize this by imagining a clock face marked with eight hours.

The two flags are held in positions that correspond to letters of the alphabet—like the hands of a clock pointing to the hours. For example, both flags held in the horizontal position represents the letter R. The user spells out a message to the receiver, who can pass it on.

A semaphore system was first used in France in 1794. The signals were made not by people holding flags, but by mechanical arms mounted on high towers. But it was essentially the same idea: the message was spelled out letter by letter. This original system was invented by an engineer named Claude Chappe. Before semaphore, it had taken 30 hours for a message to travel from Paris to Lille via horseback—now it took just a few minutes.

More semaphore lines were built in radial lines from Paris. This was, in effect, the world's first telecommunications network. Napoleon developed a portable semaphore device to enable communication among his army. "Human" semaphore with easily carried flags was the logical extension of the portable device.

The telegraph eventually rendered semaphore largely obsolete, although it remained in use in some warlike situations—for instance, in naval convoys where ships are within sight of each other but radio silence needs to be maintained. And Chappe's original semaphore still exists on the railways, where trackside signals depend on mechanical arms set to different positions.

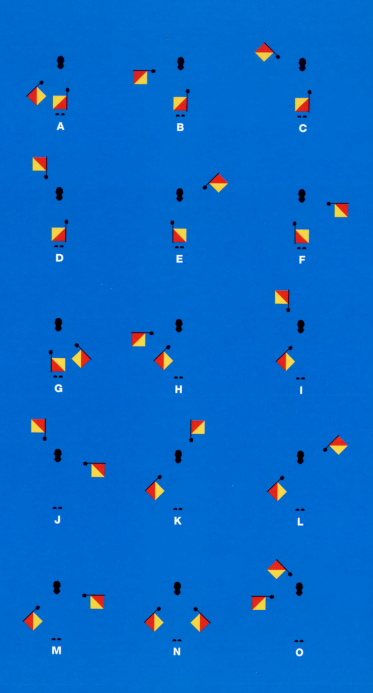

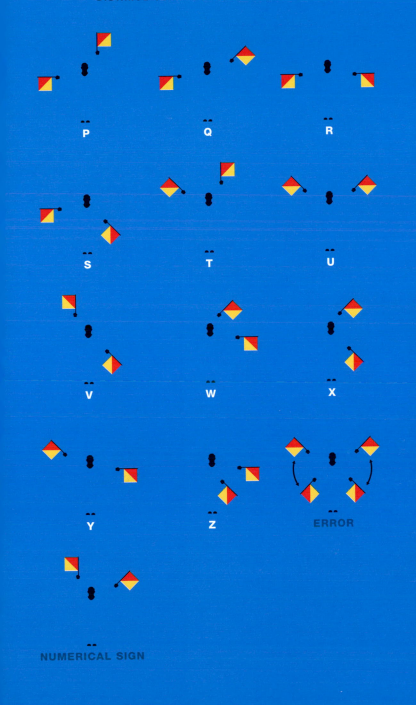

A

B

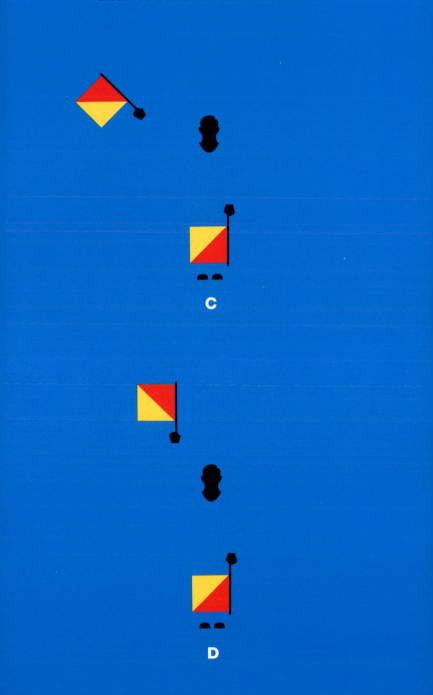

E

F

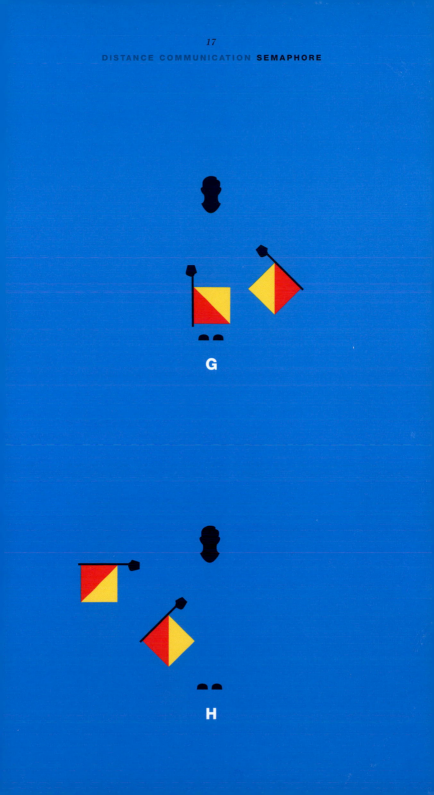

G

H

I

J

K

L

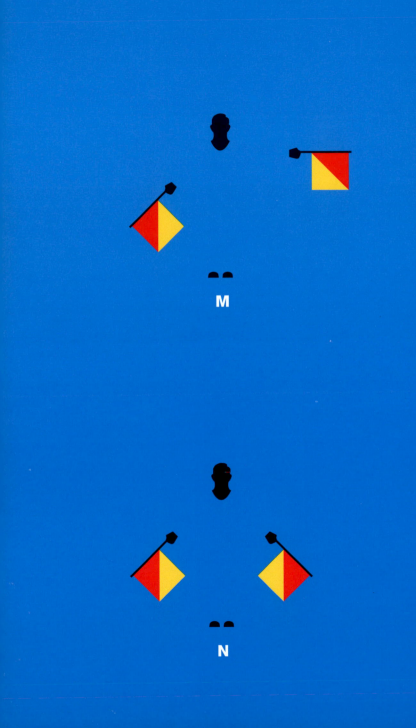

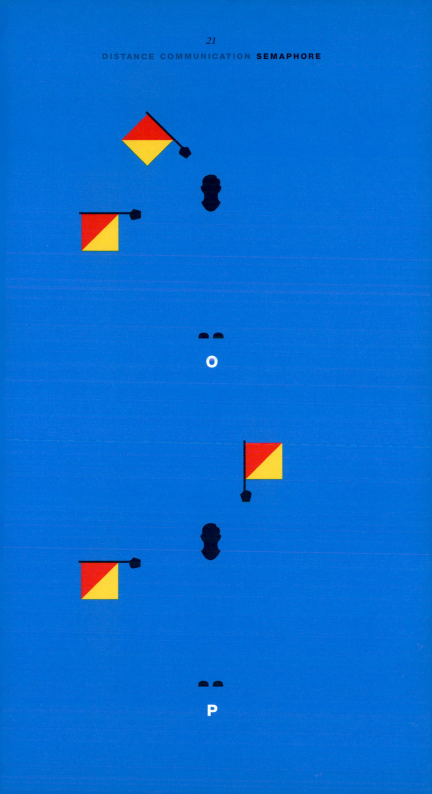

O

P

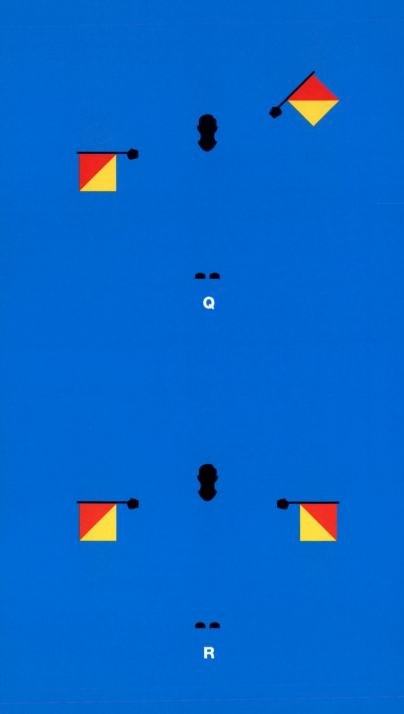

Q

R

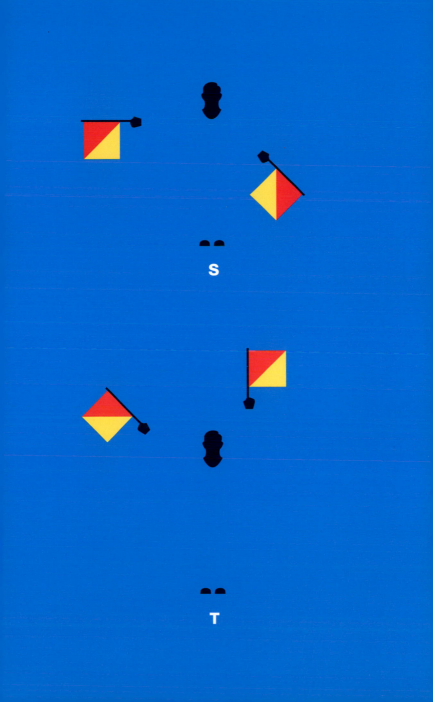

S

T

U

V

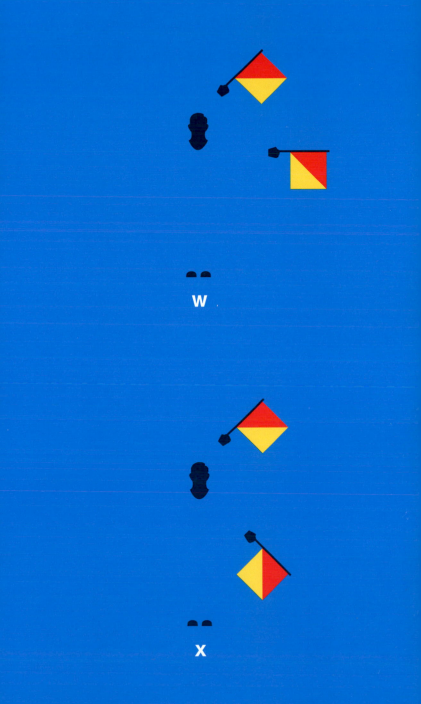

W

X

Y

Z

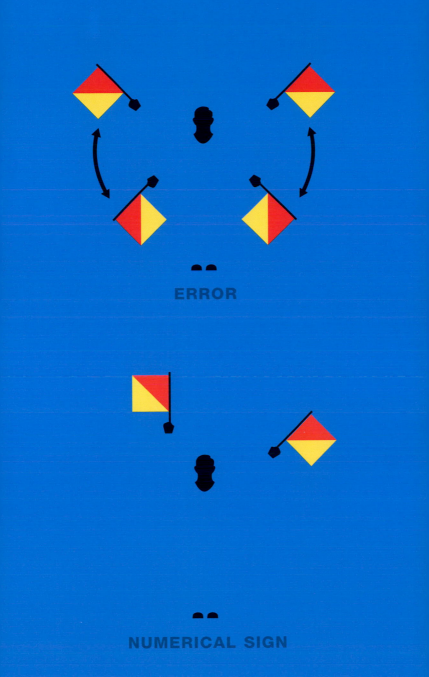

ERROR

NUMERICAL SIGN

M O R S E   C O D E

Morse code uses a system of dots and dashes to represent letters. The code is usually transmitted as electrical pulses via a telegraph wire, but it can also be sent as a visual signal using, say, a flashing light. Morse code can, in fact, be spelled out using any percussive or "on-off" device, such as tapping.

Morse code was developed by an American portrait painter, Samuel Breese Morse, who invented the electric telegraph in the late 1830s and hit on the idea of sending messages as electrical impulses along a wire. He created a telegraph key, which could be moved up or down to make or break an electrical circuit. This device could produce only a beeping sound, so he wrote the code that made it possible for intelligible messages to be transmitted. He called this American Morse Code and sent the first telegraph message from Baltimore to Washington in 1844, spelling out a rhetorical question from the Bible: "What hath God wrought?"

However, Morse realized that his original code was unwieldy, so he worked with scientist Alfred Vail to devise a more streamlined system. This new version was patented along with the telegraph itself, and became known as International Morse Code, in which each letter of the alphabet is represented by a combination of dashes and dots. A skilled Morse operator can tap out a Morse message at least as fast as it can be written in longhand.

Despite the technological advances that have been made since its appearance, Morse code remains a very reliable signaling system, although it is now more or less obsolete. In 1999, it officially ceased to be used as a means of audible communication between ships, but the SOS distress signal—standing for "Save Our Souls"—is an indelible feature of the English language. In Morse code, SOS is rendered "dot-dot-dot, dash-dash-dash, dot-dot-dot." Worth remembering: you never know when you might need it!

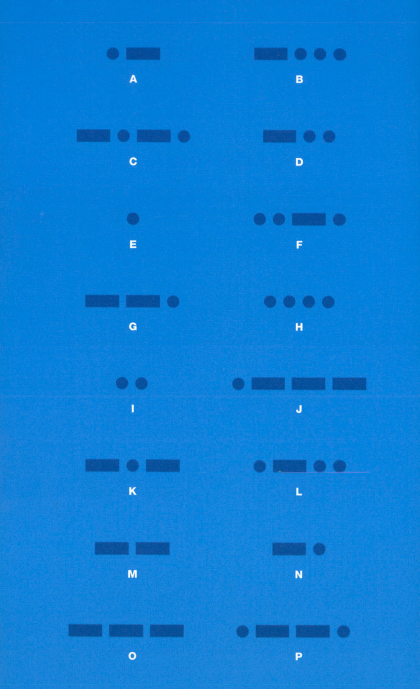

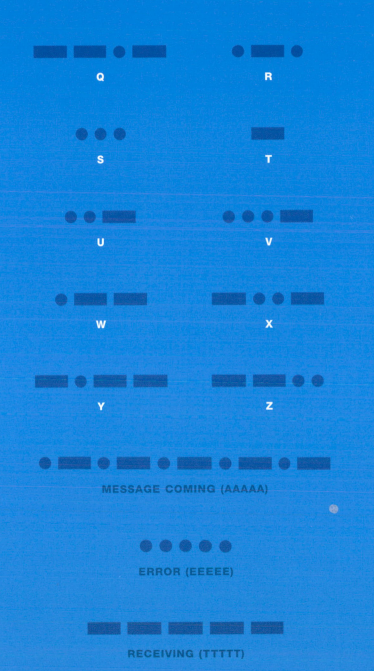

Q

R

S

T

U

V

W

X

Y

Z

MESSAGE COMING (AAAAA)

ERROR (EEEEE)

RECEIVING (TTTTT)

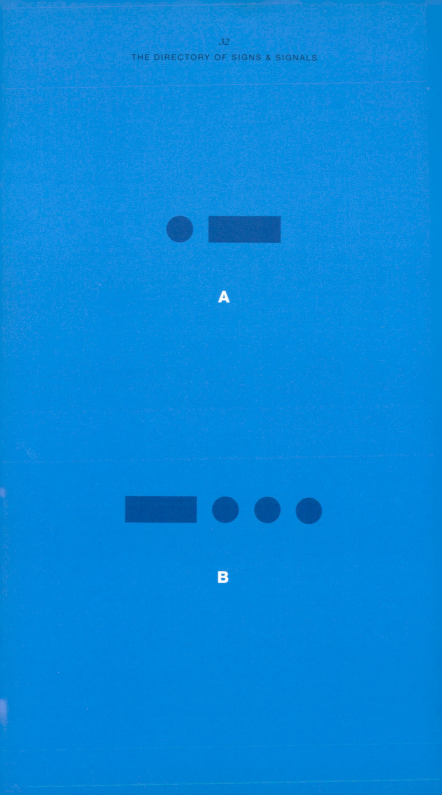

A

B

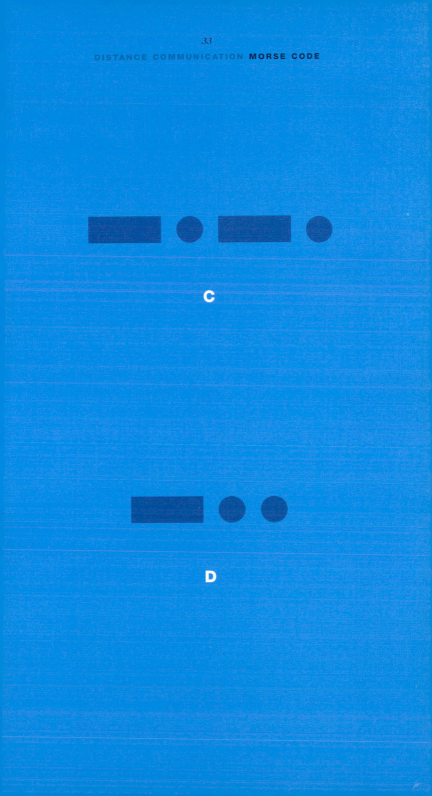

C

D

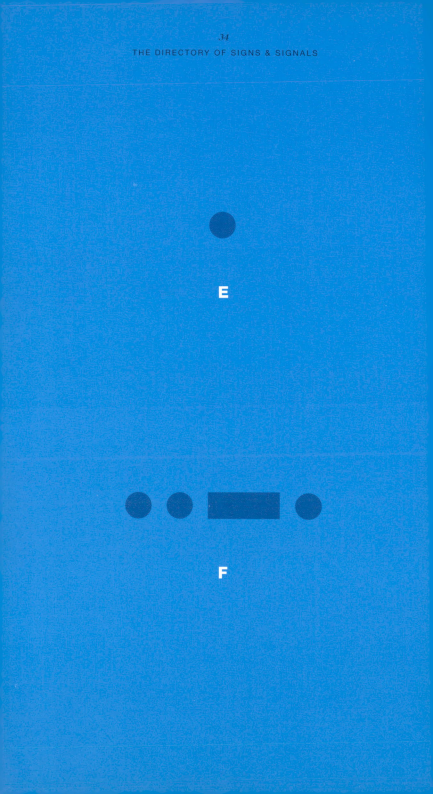

E

F

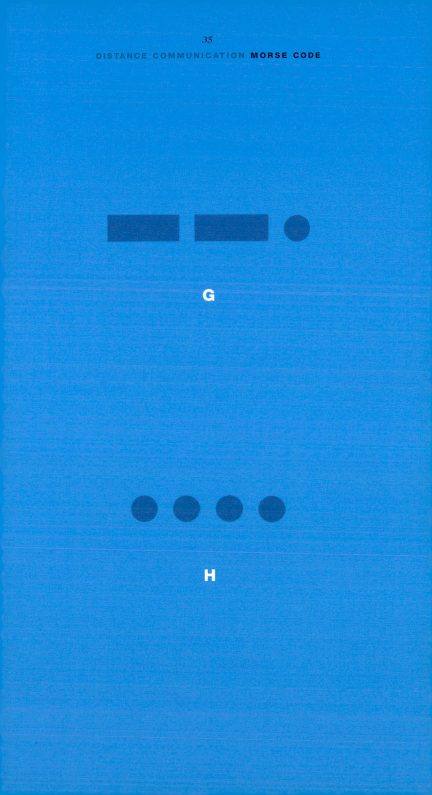

G

H

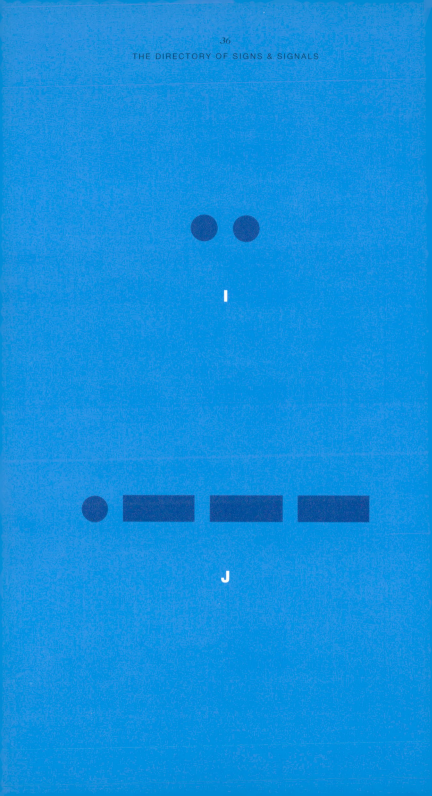

I

J

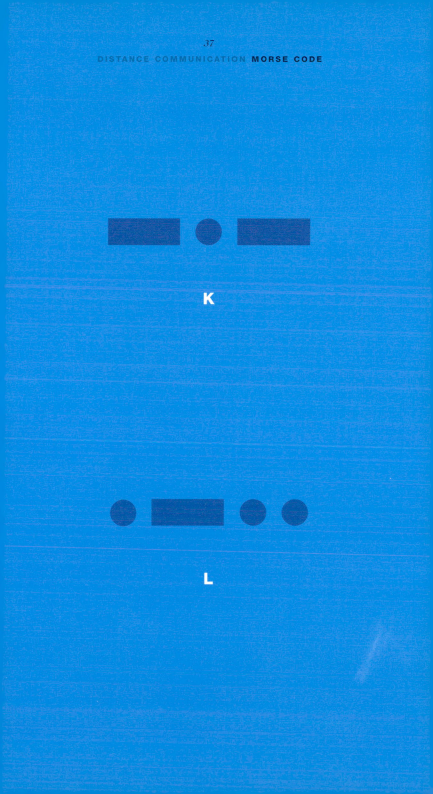

K

L

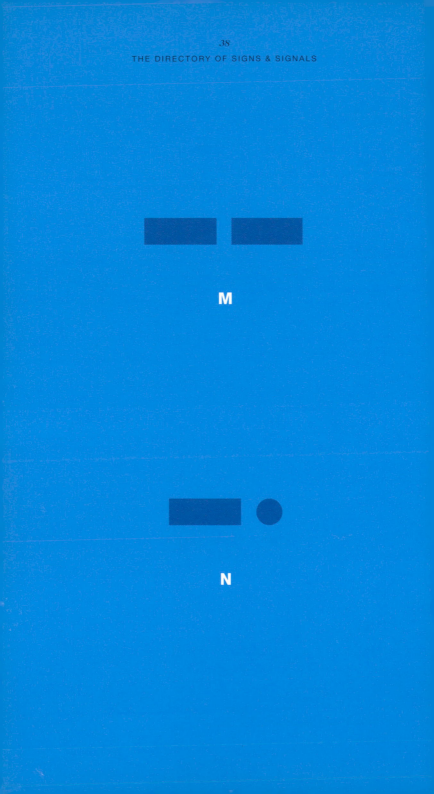

M

N

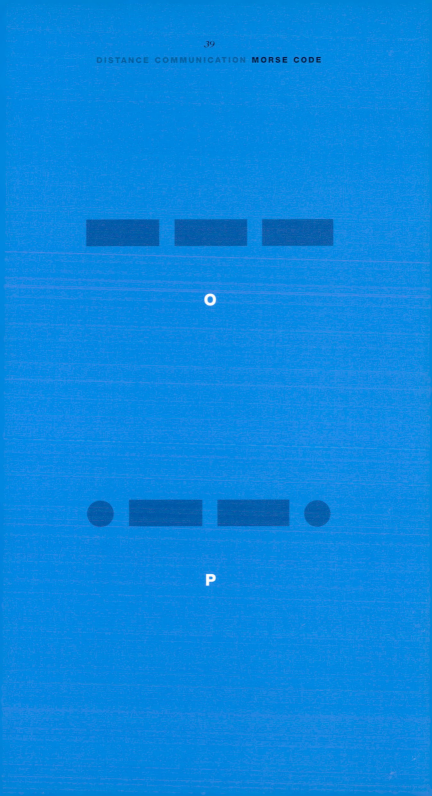

O

P

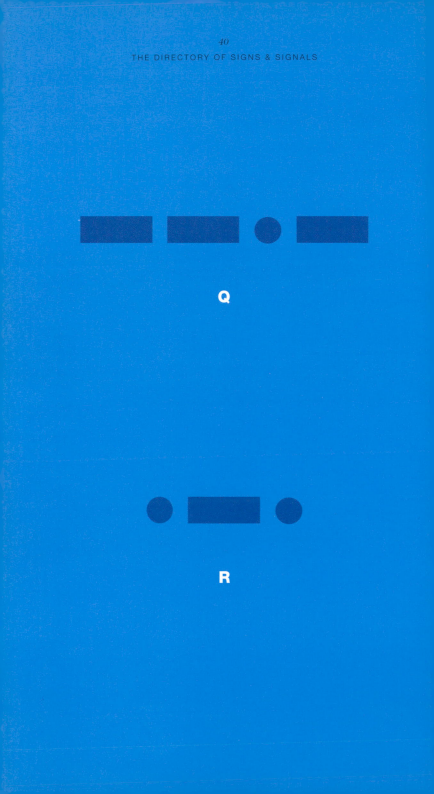

Q

R

S

T

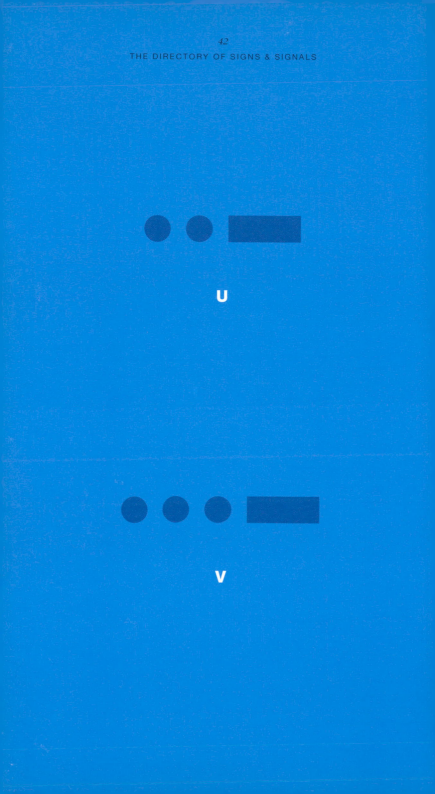

U

V

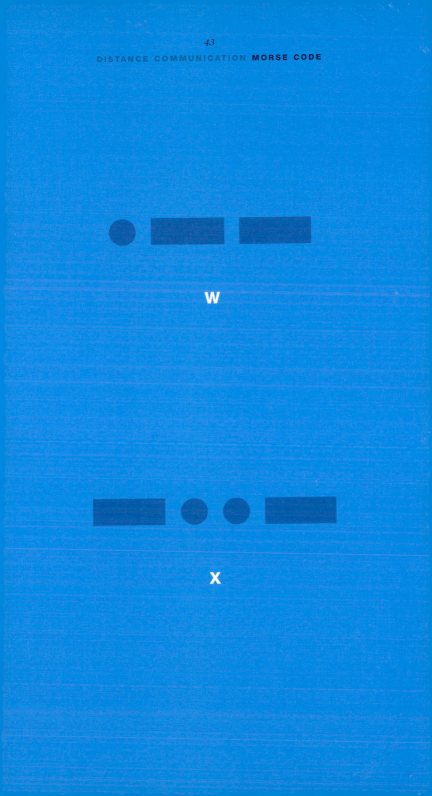

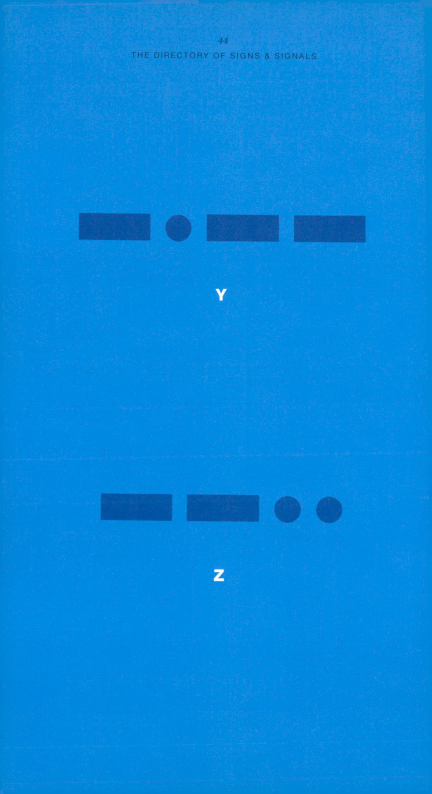

Y

Z

MESSAGE COMING
(AAAAA)

ERROR
(EEEEE)

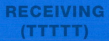

RECEIVING
(TTTTT)

MARITIME SIGNAL FLAGS

Maritime flags came into use on fighting ships in the 18th century. The British Navy had a system using nine flags, which could convey 45 fixed messages. Their meaning was laid out in a manual entitled *Permanent Fighting Instructions.* On Royal Navy flagships, the several masts were used to signal to different parts of the fleet, so that each fighting formation could be given individual directions.

During the Napoleonic Wars, the Royal Navy used a system in which flags stood for numbers. These numbers represented either specific words or directions that could be looked up in a signals book. And, for the first time, combinations of flags were assigned to letters of the alphabet. It was an efficient and economical means of communication. In Lord Nelson's famous signal at the Battle of Trafalgar— "England expects that every man will do his duty"—only the word "duty" had to be spelled out letter by letter.

In the British Navy, the code numbers assigned to each message were changed from time to time to prevent the enemy reading the signals. The American Navy, which had a similar system, was also concerned about security; it used signals books with lead plates bolted to the covers, so that if a ship was in danger of being boarded, the captain could throw them overboard to prevent their capture.

The American signaling system was the first to assign each letter of the alphabet to a single flag. These military signals were then adapted for merchant shipping in the first half of the 19th century. But the signaling system in use today is British—it was sponsored by the Board of Trade and was adopted in 1857.

The Commercial Code of Signals, as it was called, was revised in 1870 and renamed the International Code of Signals. Since 1965, the code has been administered by the United Nations' International Maritime Organization.

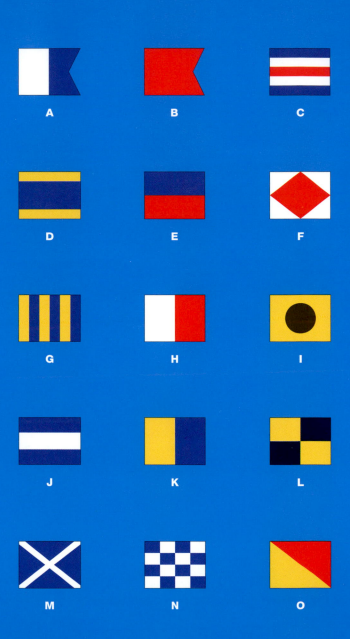

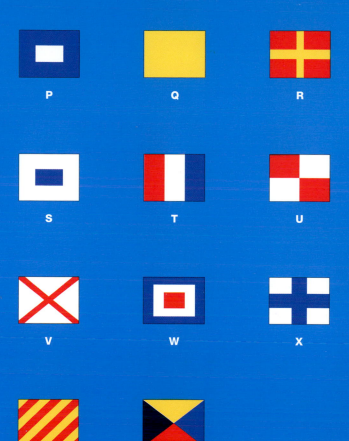

A

Undergoing speed trials

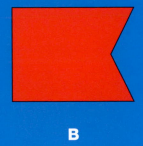

B

Explosives on board

C

Yes

D

Keep clear, I am in difficulties

E

Altering course to starboard

F

I am disabled

G

Pilot wanted

H

Pilot on board

I

Altering course to port

J

Sending message by semaphore

K

Stop at once

L

Stop, I want to communicate with you

M

Doctor on board

N

No

O

Man overboard

P

About to sail

Q

Quarantine flag

R

I have stopped

S

Going astern

T

Do not pass ahead of me

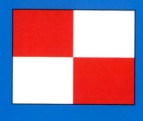

U

You are in danger

V

I need help

W

Send a doctor

X

Stop and watch for my signals

Y

Carrying mails

Z

Calling a shore station

PERSONAL
COMMUNICATION

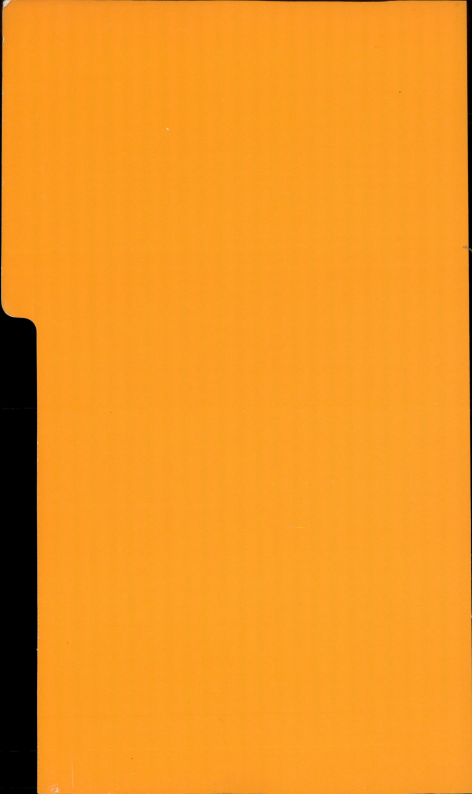

BRAILLE

**AMERICAN SIGN
LANGUAGE**

**BRITISH SIGN
LANGUAGE**

EMOTICONS

B R A I L L E

Braille is a system for reading and writing the letters of the Latin alphabet using combinations of embossed dots. These can be understood by blind people through their sense of touch. Braille was invented in 1825 by the Frenchman Louis Braille, who was blinded in an accident at the age of three. As a boy, he went to study at the Paris Blind School, where he was taught to read embossed Roman letters. However, Braille realized that the shapes of letters are meant to be apprehended visually, and that it would be much better to invent a new alphabet designed to be read by the fingertips.

Braille devised an alphabet that is based on an arbitrary system of six dots arranged in a three-by-two rectangle—like the number six on gaming dice. Each letter is represented by a combination of one or more dots in the six available positions. Braille made minor adjustments over the next few years, and by 1834 he had arrived at the system that is still in use today.

Various refinements have since been made, with a view to making the reading of Braille faster and Braille books less bulky. Chief among these is the use of contractions for very common words: for example, the letter P with a space on either side stands for "people"; and there are contractions for words like "the" and "and," and for the verb endings "-ing" and "-ed."

There are also typographic conventions which compensate for the fact that there is no upper case in Braille, and no way to vary the typeface. For instance, a piece of text centered on the page with a line space below is universally understood to be a major heading. Another innovation has been the devising of Braille code for mathematical symbols and musical notation.

Braille remains the best way of making literacy available to blind people. A practiced Braille user can read about 200 words a minute—not much slower than a sighted reader using the printed page.

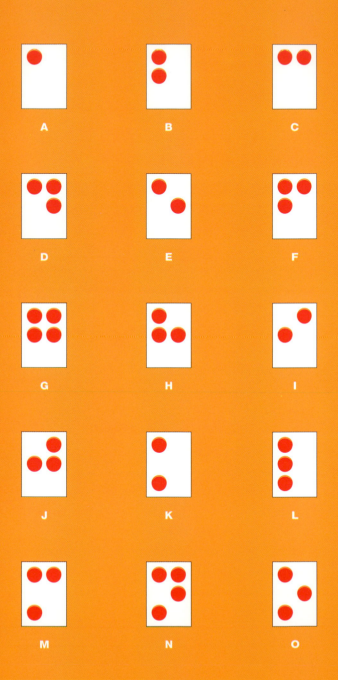

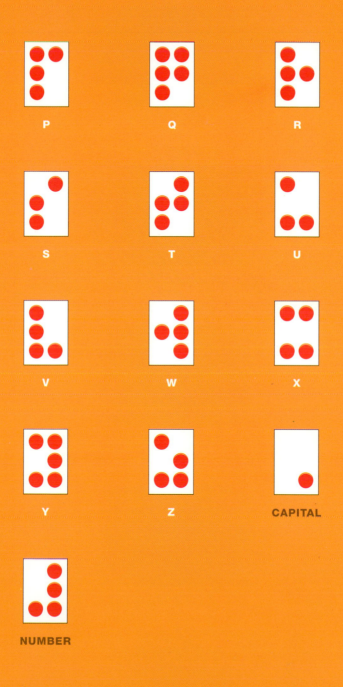

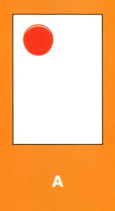

A

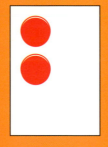

B

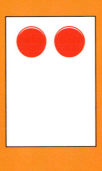

C

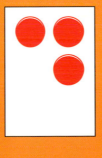

D

E

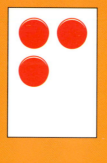

F

G

H

I

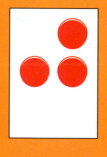

J

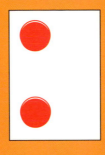

K

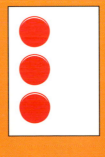

L

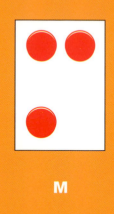

M

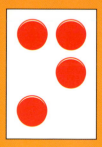

N

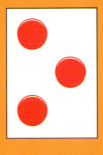

O

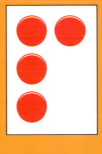

P

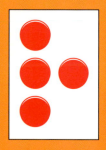

Q

R

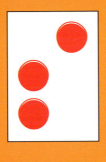

S

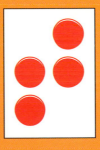

T

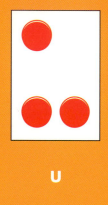

U

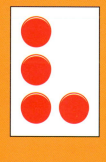

V

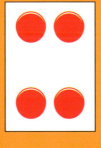

W

X

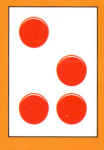

Y

Z

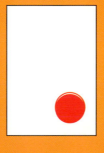

CAPITAL

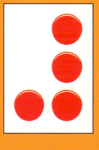

NUMBER

AMERICAN SIGN LANGUAGE

American Sign Language, known as ASL, has a hand signal corresponding to each letter of the alphabet. Yet ASL is much more than a kind of close-quarters semaphore—a way of spelling out a message to someone who cannot hear the spoken word. It is a language in every sense of the word, with a grammar, syntax, and colorful vocabulary, all of which are quite distinct from spoken or written English. Most statements in ASL are expressed through hundreds of hand signs that correspond to words, phrases, or whole sentences. The alphabet signs are used mainly for spelling out proper names, or for introducing new concepts into a discussion.

ASL is not a way of representing English, nor is it a universal language for the deaf. British Sign Language (*see pages 100–117*), for example, is quite different. An American deaf person cannot communicate with a British deaf person just by signing: their two sign languages are as mutually unintelligible as French and Russian.

Modern ASL has developed organically over many decades. One source of the modern language is the signing system used by the unusually large deaf community at Martha's Vineyard, Connecticut, in the 18th century (it seems there was a genetic propensity to deafness among some of the families there). Deaf immigrants from other parts of Europe also contributed to sign language, just as their hearing counterparts did to the English language.

A more formalized signing system was introduced by a young minister named Thomas Hopkins Gallaudet. In the mid-19th century, he developed a system based on the one used by Laurent Clerc, a deaf sign-language teacher from Paris. Together they founded schools for the deaf in the United States, where their language was taught. The system was adapted and enlarged by its users, the true "native speakers" of ASL. And, like all living languages, it continues to enrich itself with each generation of speakers.

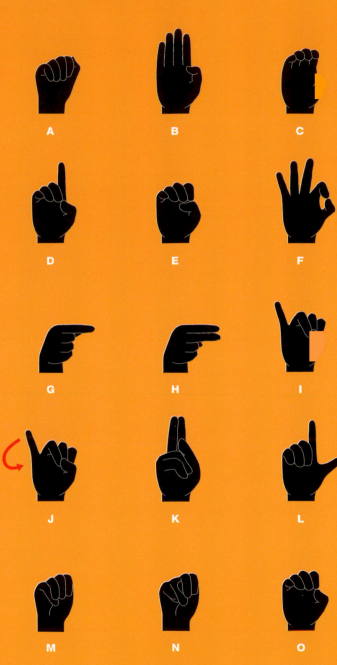

P

Q

R

S

T

U

V

W

X

Y

Z

GOOD WORK

WRONG

A

B

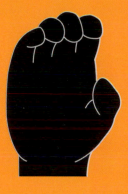

C

D

E

F

G

H

I

J

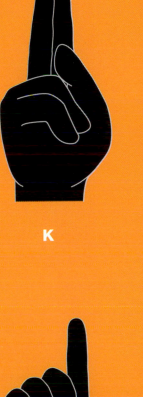

K

L

M

N

O

P

Q

R

S

T

U

V

W

X

Y

Z

GOOD WORK

WRONG

B R I T I S H
S I G N   L A N G U A G E

British Sign Language, or BSL, is an entirely autonomous language with a distinct structure and an individual character. All sign languages that are in use in the English-speaking world (American, Irish, Australian, and others) are so different from each other as to be mutually incomprehensible.

Sign language has been in use by deaf people in Britain for hundreds of years. In 1595, in his *Survey of Cornwall*, Richard Carew noted a signed conversation between two deaf people. Even before that, in 1576, the Parish Book of St Martin's in Leicester recorded a wedding ceremony conducted partly in sign language. But the first work to devote more than a passing reference to the use of sign language in Britain was John Bulwer's *Chirologia—the National Language of the Hand*, written in 1644.

The word "chirologia" was Bulwer's coinage from the Greek and means "hand-speech." But sign language has always been more than a system of sophisticated gesturing. It would be more correct to call it "visual speech": apart from hand signs, modern BSL uses facial expressions, lip patterns, head movements, and orientation of the upper body to alter a sentence's meaning.

During the 19th century, the use of sign language was officially discouraged in Britain. Educators took the view that the use of sign language prevented deaf children from acquiring lip-reading skills, which were considered more socially useful. The British Deaf Association was founded in 1890 to press for the continued teaching of sign language in schools and to promote its use as the ordinary language of discourse between deaf people.

However, the term BSL was not coined until 1975, and the first BSL–English dictionary was published only in 1992. There are now around 70,000 people in Britain who look on BSL as their first or preferred language—almost as many users as there are speakers of Welsh.

A

B

C

D

E

F

G

H

I

J

K

L

M

N

O

P

Q

R

S

T

U

V

W

X

Y

Z

CORRECTION

EXCELLENT

A

B

C

D

E

F

G

H

I

J

K

L

M

N

O

P

Q

R

S

T

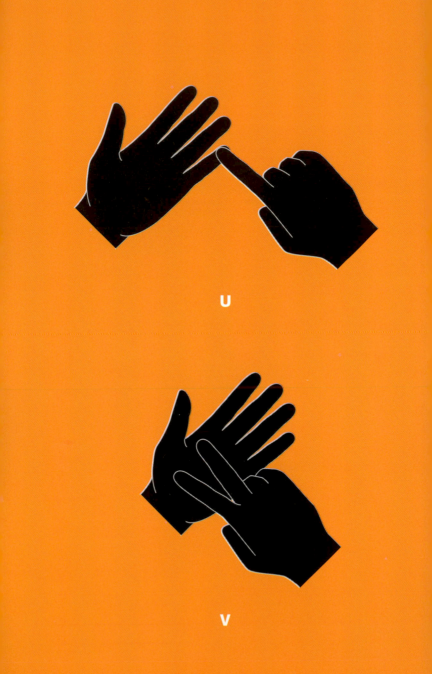

U

V

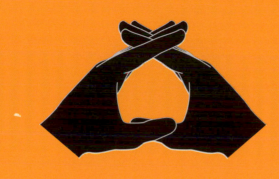

W

X

Y

Z

CORRECTION

EXCELLENT

EMOTICONS

Emoticons are small representations of the human face, constructed from letters of the alphabet and from punctuation. They are used in e-mail messages to convey the state of mind of the person who is writing.

The speed and informality of e-mail can sometimes lead to confusion—something may be dashed off in jest, or meant ironically, but that intention may not be clear to the recipient. So emoticons function like a kind of emotional punctuation: if you say to someone, "I think you need psychiatric help," then a smiley icon at the end makes it clear that you are only joking.

Emoticons usually have to be "read" sideways. The most basic ones use a colon or a semicolon to represent the eyes, a dash for the nose, and a variety of typographical symbols to portray the mouth: smiling, skeptical, tongue-tied, yawning.

In the early days of e-mail and word processing, computers were able to generate only 256 separate characters, called ASCII characters (standing for American Standard Code for Information Interchange). A great deal of ingenuity was invested in constructing witty and comprehensible representations of the human face using this limited palette.

Then people realized that it was possible to construct more complex images using the standard 256 characters. This outgrowth of the emoticon became known as "ASCII art," and for a short while there was a craze for e-mailing complex typographical renditions of the *Mona Lisa* and so on. But ASCII art worked only while all computers shared the same primitive settings. It practically ceased to exist once people could set such variables as their own fonts and line spacing.

However, simple emoticons live on, albeit in a more sophisticated form. Today, if you type a colon, a dash, and a right bracket into a word-processing program, it will automatically be rendered as a smiling face—turned the right way up.

HAPPY

LAUGHING

SKEPTICAL

MY LIPS ARE SEALED

<:-(

ANGRY

:-@

SCREAMING

INDIFFERENT

YAWNING

:-&

TONGUE-TIED

KISSING

SURVIVAL

K

GROUND-TO-AIR
SIGNALS

BODY SIGNALS

TRAIL SIGNS

GROUND-TO-AIR SIGNALS

Ground-to-air signals are used to convey information to airplanes or helicopters. If you are lost, injured, or ill, then it is important to communicate this in the instant you are spotted by rescuers. It can, in fact, mean the difference between life and death.

The basic ground-to-air symbols are few, simple, and easy to learn. Professional outdoor people, such as the soldiers of the SAS, carry fluorescent strips that can be laid out on the ground to make these symbols. However, they can be constructed from any available material, as long as the result is visible from the air.

A stranded skier, for example, might tramp out a signal in undisturbed snow—this shows up surprisingly well. Someone who is lost in open moorland might cut a trough in the ground, while someone marooned on a mountainside might build a symbol from stones. Anything that is to hand (branches of trees, bits of wreckage, footprints in the sand) can be used to make the signal, as long as it contrasts with the background and is large enough to be discernible from the air. Heaping earth or some other material on one side of your signal makes it more likely that it will be spotted in the morning or evening because of its long shadow. But all that matters is that the symbols are clearly depicted, and that they are big enough to be seen and understood. Ground symbols should be at least 20 feet/6 meters long and rendered in lines at least 3¼ feet/1 meter thick.

If you are stranded, you should do everything you can think of to draw attention to your signal, such as making a pile of brightly colored objects: clothes, colored wreckage, and so on. A fire attracts attention because both flame and smoke can be seen a long way off. Light smoke stands out against dark earth or in a forest, so stoke your fire with green grass, leaves, and ferns; dark smoke shows up well against snow or sand, so use oil or rubber, if these are available.

REQUIRE DOCTOR

**REQUIRE
MEDICAL SUPPLIES**

UNABLE TO PROCEED

**REQUIRE
FOOD / WATER**

**REQUIRE FIREARMS
/ AMMUNITION**

**REQUIRE
MAP / COMPASS**

REQUIRE
SIGNAL LAMP

INDICATE DIRECTION
TO PROCEED

**PROCEEDING IN
THIS DIRECTION**

**WILL ATTEMPT
TAKE-OFF**

AIRCRAFT
BADLY DAMAGED

PROBABLY SAFE
TO LAND HERE

REQUIRE FUEL / OIL

ALL IS WELL

ꓕ

NOT UNDERSTOOD

W

REQUIRE MECHANIC

B O D Y   S I G N A L S

A stranded person can communicate with an airplane using a set of body signals. These are understood internationally. They involve moving the whole body in an exaggerated and deliberate way, so that the signal can be easily understood from above and at a distance.

A limited range of signs is used, but they cover most emergency situations. For example, you can communicate your need for a radio or a mechanic; signal that you are ill or injured; or let an airplane know where it can land for a rescue mission. Body signals include simple arm gestures that signify "yes" and "no." It is best to hold a cloth in the hand when performing these gestures, since this makes the movements easier to spot.

The pilot of an airplane can acknowledge the signals from the ground by maneuvering the aircraft in a particular way. In effect, the airplane makes wing gestures. Tipping the wings of the plane from side to side means "message received

and understood" (at night, flashing green lights
are used). Flying the plane in a right-handed
circle (or at night, flashing red lights) means
"message received, but not understood."

Body signals can also be used in combat
situations by military personnel, although from
a fast-moving airplane it can be almost impos-
sible to identify friendly front-line troops. For
this reason, infantry troops in modern warfare
always carry a "panel marker"—something such
as a flag or a unit badge, which can be displayed
on the ground in a way that is visible to a pilot.

When someone is lost in a sparsely populated
region, flares can be used as visual signals. A red
flare always indicates "SOS"; a white flare "message
understood." Distress can also be conveyed using
any sound or light source: six blasts of a horn or
flashes of a torch in quick succession are the
common mountain-rescue sign for "help needed."
Once you have attracted attention, body signals
can give more information, if necessary.

PICK US UP

ALL IS WELL

NEED MECHANICAL HELP

NEED MEDICAL ASSISTANCE

LAND HERE

**DON'T ATTEMPT
TO LAND HERE**

DROP MESSAGE

HAVE RADIO

YES

NO

MESSAGE RECEIVED
AND UNDERSTOOD

MESSAGE RECEIVED,
NOT UNDERSTOOD

T R A I L   S I G N S

Trail signs are a means of indicating to others where you have gone when you are out in the open. They could be useful in a rescue situation where, for example, you might have left the scene of a wreck to look for food or shelter. But they are more generally used in less dramatic situations: to point the way forward for stragglers or following groups in a trekking party.

Trail signs are made on the ground, usually close to the left-hand side of the trail. This convention makes it easier for those who are following the signs to spot them. Most of the signs are directional: the stones, sticks, bent bushes, and knotted sheaves of grass that are used to make the signs are all simply arrows of one sort or another. The various means of creating the arrows allow the signer to make use of the terrain and the materials that are to hand. All trail signs are designed to convey a particular message without causing lasting damage either to property or to the environment.

The traditional smoke signals used by the Native American peoples are a form of trail sign. In a simple form, some of these are still used in the United States. One steady smoke means "here is camp;" two steady smokes, from two fires side-by-side, means "I am lost, come and help me."

The chalked signals used by tramps and hoboes in the first part of the 20th century are a kind of urban variant of the old trail signs. They were intended not to show the way, but to share useful experience. In America, an X on a gatepost meant that the owner of the house was a man, while an inverted Y denoted a woman; a T-shape meant "makes you work for meals," whereas a spiral signified "pass by: policeman lives here."

In England there was a different vocabulary of signs. An X, for example, meant "too poor to give anything" and a cross inside a circle meant "religious, but kind."

THIS WAY

THIS WAY

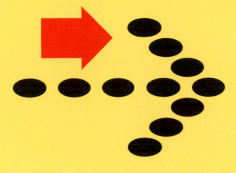

THIS WAY

THIS IS THE TRAIL

CHANGE DIRECTION

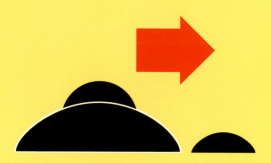

CHANGE DIRECTION

CHANGE DIRECTION

NOT THIS WAY

DANGER

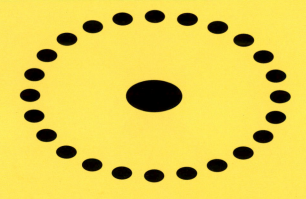

GONE HOME

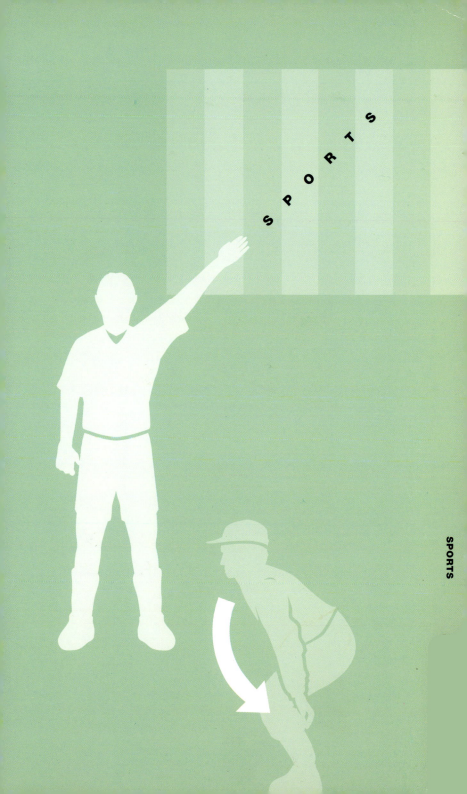

SPORTS

**AMERICAN FOOTBALL
HAND SIGNALS**

**SOCCER HAND
SIGNALS**

**MOTOR-RACING
FLAGS**

AMERICAN FOOTBALL HAND SIGNALS

American football developed in the United States in the 19th century, borrowing elements from both soccer and rugby. But despite a superficial resemblance to both games, modern American football is a very different sport from its two European antecedents.

The simple aim of American football is to gain territory on the field by moving the ball forward, and to carry the ball in the opponents' endzone to score a touchdown. This forward progress is achieved through a series of set-piece "plays," which are governed by a set of highly complex rules. The regulations cover everything from equipment (it is illegal for a player to remove his helmet after a touchdown) to crowd noise (uniquely in the world of sport, a team can be penalized if its supporters are making too much of a din).

These infringements, and many others, are indicated by a wide-ranging vocabulary of signals. These gestures are more expansive than in most other sports, such as soccer, where simple hand gestures suffice. In American football referees bend, strike their thighs or the back of the calves, use their legs to mime a trip, and clasp their head in their hands.

Some of the signals are composite. A personal foul is indicated by one wrist striking the other above the head, and the exact nature of the foul is demonstrated by a separate movement performed immediately afterward: a swinging leg means "roughing the kicker" and a raised arm swinging forward means "roughing the passer."

The person whose job it is to make the signals is the referee. In professional games there are six other officials. Each of them has a highly specialized role in overseeing the game, and is in constant visual contact with the referee. All the members of the officiating crew wear a uniform consisting of a shirt with vertical black-and-white stripes, white trousers, and a white or black hat.

TOUCHDOWN

TIME OUT

(Referee's time out when followed
by one hand on top of cap)

ILLEGAL BLOCK
BELOW THE WAIST

FIRST DOWN

FOURTH DOWN

(Crowd noise with open hand)

BALL ILLEGALLY TOUCHED

NO TIME OUT

DELAY OF GAME

FALSE START

PERSONAL FOUL

HOLDING

ILLEGAL USE
OF HANDS OR BODY

**PENALTY
REFUSED**

**PASS JUGGLED
INBOUNDS**

**ILLEGAL
FORWARD PASS**

INVALID
FAIR CATCH

INTERFERENCE WITH
FORWARD PASS

INTENTIONAL
GROUNDING OF PASS

**INELIGIBLE
RECEIVER**

**ILLEGAL
CONTACT**

OFFSIDE

ILLEGAL MOTION
AT SNAP

LOSS OF DOWN

INTERLOCKING
INTERFERENCE

UNSPORTSMANLIKE
CONDUCT

TOUCHING A
FORWARD PASS

ILLEGAL CUT

ILLEGAL CRACKBACK

PLAYER DISQUALIFIED

TRIPPING

UNCATCHABLE
FORWARD PASS

TWELVE MEN
IN OFFENSIVE HUDDLE

FACE MASK

(Major face mask when preceded by personal foul sign)

ILLEGAL SHIFT

**RESET PLAY CLOCK:
25 SECONDS**

**RESET PLAY CLOCK:
40 SECONDS**

SAFETY

**ROUGHING
THE KICKER**

**ROUGHING
THE PASSER**

CHOP BLOCK

CLIPPING

TOUCHBACK

S O C C E R

H A N D   S I G N A L S

In soccer, signals are made both by the referee and by the two referee's assistants (formerly known as linesmen). The function of the signals is to enable the officials to communicate with each other; and to let the players and the spectators know what decisions are being made, and why.

The use of yellow and red cards to indicate bookings and sendings-off is a relatively recent innovation. The idea belongs to Ken Aston, a British official who refereed a violent and bad-tempered game between Chile and Italy in the 1962 World Cup. The language barrier had made it difficult for Aston to dismiss players, so afterward he suggested to FIFA (football's governing body) that it should adopt a nonverbal signal for bookings in international matches. The cards were introduced at the 1970 World Cup in Mexico and had a salutary effect on discipline: no one was sent off in the course of that tournament—the red card was not used once.

The quarrelsome behavior of professional footballers has given rise to a number of discreet, unofficial signals between referees and assistants. For example, an assistant referee may subtly point to the red or yellow square on his flag to indicate whether he thinks the referee should punish an offence with a sending-off or a booking. Such signals enable assistants to disagree with a referee, or to offer an opinion, without appearing to undermine his authority, although they became less useful once players came to recognize them.

There are other less contentious signals that a referee can make to his assistants. In the crucial last minutes of a game, or after a dispute between teams, he may make a clenched fist at his side. This indicates that he intends to govern the game strictly for the next 10 minutes, and that his assistants should follow suit. If he makes a gesture with outstretched fingers at his side, this means the strict interlude is over.

CAUTION

SENDING-OFF

CORNER

GOAL KICK

PENALTY

ADVANTAGE

INDIRECT FREE KICK

DIRECT FREE KICK

THROW-IN

ATTENTION REFEREE

OFFSIDE

CORNER

GOAL KICK

**THROW-IN TO TEAM
KICKING RIGHT**

**THROW-IN TO TEAM
KICKING LEFT**

PENALTY

BALL OUT OF PLAY

SUBSTITUTE

MOTOR-RACING
FLAGS

Motor-racing flags are used to let drivers know about the condition of the track ahead. Each flag has a precise meaning, which can vary depending on how it is displayed. Such versatility is important with the yellow flag, which signals danger. A single waving yellow flag indicates a hazard either on the track surface or somewhere near it; two waving yellow flags are used when more than half of the track is blocked. When a single yellow flag is held steady, this signifies that the hazard is likely to persist for the duration of the race; two steady yellow flags are displayed when the hazard extends across the whole course.

The black flag, indicating a compulsory pitstop, is never waved: it is only ever displayed in steady fashion, usually together with the number of the car that is to stop.

No one knows the exact origin of the black-and-white checkered flag: some say that it derives from horse-racing, yachting, or bicycling;

others that it comes from heraldry or naval signals. All of these explanations are unlikely. It has been pointed out that, at the medieval festival of horses in Ferrara, Italy, the finish line was marked by a black-and-white flag. If this was the origin of today's checkered flag, there is still no explanation of how the flag came to be adopted in the age of the internal-combustion engine. All that is known for certain is that the flag has been in use since at least 1904—almost as long as there have been cars to race.

However, flags are not the only use of color signals in motor racing. When Formula One racing began after World War II, each of the participating nations was identified by a color. French cars were blue, the German ones were silver, the Italians red, and the British green. In Britain this custom gave rise to the term "racing green," which now denotes a particular shade of the color (in the same way as lincoln green or navy blue).

CAUTION,
DANGER AHEAD

OIL ON TRACK

MUST CALL
IN AT PIT

RACE MUST STOP

LET FASTER
DRIVER OVERTAKE

AMBULANCE OR
OTHER OFFICIAL
VEHICLE ON TRACK

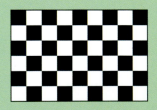

FINISH

MISCELLANEOUS

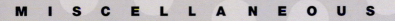

TRADING SIGNALS

WEATHER SYMBOLS

T R A D I N G   S I G N A L S

Trading floors are noisy, crowded places, but they are also places where it is important to convey information quickly: a half-minute delay can make the difference between clinching a lucrative deal or seeing it slip away. For this reason, traders on stock-market floors around the world have developed signaling systems. Their signals enable them to buy and sell, make offers, and convey precise information about currencies, account numbers, money amounts, and all the complex issues that affect transactions in areas such as futures.

All this can be done across a heaving trading floor, at a distance of tens of yards, without exchanging a word. Hand gestures and facial expressions are used to convey meaning. It is, in effect, a sign language such as that used by the deaf, but one with a limited vocabulary and a special emphasis on dates and figures. The language of the trading floor is closely related to the tic-tac signals used by bookies at race courses.

However, the sign language of the stock markets is not dry, visual mathematics. Many of the signs are full of punning wit and ribaldry—partly because this form of trading is traditionally the province of competitive young men. On the Chicago Stock Exchange, a trader alerts the market to the fact that he is interested in pounds by banging his fist (pounding) on his head; the sign for French francs (before they became extinct) involved a lascivious gesture with the tongue.

The same signs can have vastly differing meanings in different exchanges—or even in different trading pits within the same exchange. For example, a forefinger and little finger pointed toward the floor stands for the letter M, but—depending on the location and context—it could mean Merrill Lynch, Morgan Stanley, or, bizarrely, the month of June. Entire careers (and small fortunes) can depend on reading the signal correctly.

BUY

SELL

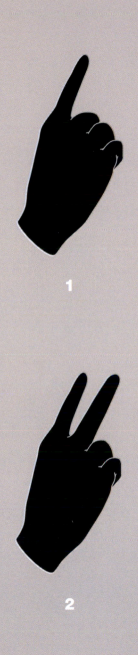

1

2

3

4

5

6

7

8

9

EVEN

FILLED

WORKING

STOP

CANCEL

✳ ✳
WEATHER
SYMBOLS

The signs used by professional meteorologists to plot the weather on a map are very different from those used in television forecasts destined for the general public. Meteorologists have evolved a system of signs that enables them to combine various bits of information—cloud cover, amount and type of precipitation, temperature, air pressure—into one composite sketch. This sketch, called a "station model," gives a complete rundown of the state of the weather as plotted at one weather station on the ground. It is then plotted on a map, together with the station models from other points across a region or an entire country.

The center of any station model is a circle representing cloud cover. The more of the circle that is colored in, the greater the amount of cloud over that point. Wind direction is shown with a stylized arrow pointing like a compass in the direction from which the wind is blowing. A system of "barbs," little notches drawn on the tail of the arrow, conveys the speed of the wind: broadly speaking, the more barbs on the arrow, the stronger the wind.

Rain is depicted by dots to the left of the circle. The heavier the rain, the more dots (up to a maximum of four). The same system is used for snow, which is depicted by an asterisk, like a stylized snowflake. A warm front is represented by a continuous red line hung with half-moons; a cold front by a blue line with triangles— perhaps a far-fetched depiction of an icicle. Air temperature and barometric pressure are written as figures around the station model. Air temperature is always shown to the top and left.

These conventions mean that an experienced meteorologist can run an eye over a map full of station models and understand it instantly. Just as a musician scans a score and can hear the music in his head, so a meteorologist can gain a snapshot impression of the state of the weather over a vast area and how it is likely to develop.

WIND

Blowing from the south at 5 knots

WIND

Blowing from the northeast at 25 knots

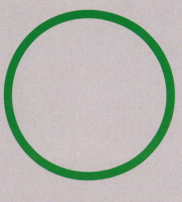

CLOUD COVER

Clear

CLOUD COVER

Mostly cloudy (about 75% cloud cover)

RAIN

Light

RAIN

Heavy

DRIZZLE

Light

DRIZZLE

Heavy

SNOW

Light

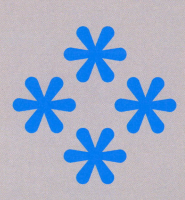

SNOW

Heavy

RAIN SHOWER

Light

SNOW SHOWER

Moderate

FREEZING DRIZZLE

Light

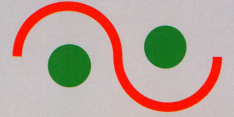

FREEZING RAIN

Moderate

HAIL

Moderate or heavy hail or ice pellets

HAIL

Light hail or ice-pellet shower

THUNDERSTORM

THUNDERSTORM

Severe

THUNDERSTORM

With hail

SNOW

Drifting or blowing

HAZE

FOG

SMOKE

DUST STORM

TORNADO OR
FUNNEL CLOUD

HURRICANE

COLD FRONT

WARM FRONT

I N D E X